Anonymous

Ontario as a Home for the British Tenant Farmer

Who Desires to Become His Own Landlord

Anonymous

Ontario as a Home for the British Tenant Farmer
Who Desires to Become His Own Landlord

ISBN/EAN: 9783337314729

Printed in Europe, USA, Canada, Australia, Japan

Cover: Foto ©Suzi / pixelio.de

More available books at **www.hansebooks.com**

ONTARIO

AS A HOME FOR THE

BRITISH TENANT FARMER

WHO DESIRES TO BECOME

HIS OWN LANDLORD.

[NEW EDITION, REVISED AND CORRECTED TO DATE.]

ISSUED BY AUTHORITY OF THE GOVERNMENT OF ONTARIO.

HON. JOHN DRYDEN, M.P.P.,
Commissioner of Immigration.

DAVID SPENCE,
Secretary, Immigration Department.

TORONTO:

PRINTED BY WARWICK & SONS, 68 AND 70 FRONT STREET WEST,
1892.

CONTENTS.

.

CONTENTS.

—

INTRODUCTION.

The Dominion of Canada offers to the surplus population of the British Isles ample opportunities for the betterment of their condition in various walks of enterprise and industry, and its several Provinces possess diverse attractions as well as many features in common. When, therefore, the intending emigrant has decided to make his future home in Canada, the question arises as to which locality within its vast domain he should betake himself. The choice depends upon so many contingencies that each one must determine it according to his own circumstances and predilections; but the facts set forth in the following pages prove that for the tenant farmers, farm labourers and all who desire to devote themselves to agricultural industry, and transfer their energies and (those who have it) their capital to the New World, there are many special advantages offered by the Province of Ontario.

In this Province substantial wealth, or a reasonable competency, is within the reach of every industrious man whose efforts are intelligently directed. The penniless pioneer of a few years ago is the substantial, independent farmer of to-day. The uplifting of the people in social and material comfort is a process as visibly going on from year to year as the revolution of the seasons. Its progress is recorded in the annual advance in the value of accumulated property, in the increase of trade, in the establishment and development of religious, educational and benevolent institutions, in the spread of social refinement, in the cultivation of the sciences in the appliance of every art that ministers to the happiness of human life. Nor are these conditions the result of long and painful evolution, taking generations for their development. The young man with no capital, if possessing only an average knowledge of agricultural labour, and devoting himself earnestly to work, may, with the exercise of reasonable economy, realize a competence by the time he has reached middle life; and the man who is a practical farmer and the possessor of means sufficient to stock an average English farm, can at once begin life in Ontario as his own landlord, with every assurance of a prosperous career before him.

The present condition of agricultural industry in the British Isles offers no such encouraging prospects either to the labourer or the farmer with limited capital. Where the cultivable area is so small and the population is so dense, the most liberal land laws cannot counteract the lowering influences of competition, and against these influences only the few can hope to rise above the average level, which will always be below the normal condition of the same class in a country wherein land is plentiful, and its ownership of easy acquisition. In the Province of Ontario the farm labourer can, in a few years gather means enough to rent a farm ; in a few years more, by well-directed industry, he will, under ordinary circumstances, be in a position to buy one for himself. The farmer with moderate means can begin at once as his own landlord ; or, if he prefers to acquire a little experience and personal knowledge of the country before making a permanent investment he can rent for a short term, until he has had time to make up his mind as to the locality in which he would like to " settle down."

It is because of these opportunities that Ontario is an exceptionally attractive field. It offers all the advantages of the New World, combined with the least sense of deprivation of the comforts of the Old, and to the emigrant from Great Britain or Ireland the most congenial and home like surroundings, with unrivalled facilities for establishing himself in comfort and independence.

THE PROVINCE OF ONTARIO.

EXTENT AND GEOGRAPHICAL POSITION.

Ontario embraces an area of nearly two hundred thousand square miles, about eighty thousand more than the United Kingdom. It extends from east to west nearly eleven hundred miles, and from north to south seven hundred miles. Its southern border, Essex County, on the shores of Lake Erie, is traversed by the 42nd parallel, and its northern, at James Bay (forming the southern extremity of Hudson's Bay) by the 52nd, so that it lies within the same degrees of latitude as Michigan, New York, and the New England States, as well as the greater portion of the most fertile countries in Europe. The international boundary line, dividing Canada from the United States, which runs through the River St. Lawrence and the great chain of lakes, Ontario, Erie, Huron and Superior, forms the southern and south-western boundary of the Province ; on the west lies the Province of Manitoba ; on the north the District of Keewatin and James' Bay, and north-easterly the Ottawa River divides it from Quebec, the latter Province forming the eastern boundary.

WATER SUPPLY.

It is bountifully supplied with water throughout its whole extent ; there are patches of swamp land in some districts, but they are usually of small dimensions, and though little fitted for the purposes of agriculture, are exceedingly valuable to a neighborhood on account of the durability of their timber, which is specially adapted for the making of shingles, posts, fence rails, paving-blocks, etc., etc. But nowhere is there an arid district, or one in which an abundant water-supply cannot be readily procured, both for man and beast. Besides innumerable lakes, rivers, creeks and streamlets, springs abound in many localities, and everywhere under the soil pure, wholesome water can be "struck" at distances varying from fourteen to forty feet, so that sinking a well, which is frequently a necessity for an isolated household, is very seldom attended with very much trouble or great expense.

NATURAL WEALTH.

Ontario's vast wealth of timber is still one of its most valuable heritages, capable of furnishing an abundant supply, both for home consumption and

for every probable demand that commerce can make upon it for generations to come. The great region which is the main depository of nature's
most liberal gifts in mineral wealth is as yet only partially explored. But
it is established beyond doubt that the Districts of Algoma, Nipissing,
Thunder Bay and Rainy River are enormously rich in nickel, iron, silver,
copper and many other minerals. In the Ottawa region, in addition to
these, there have been considerable finds of gold, while the quarrying of
plaster of paris or gypsum, phosphates, mica, asbestos, etc., and marble
of excellent quality are profitable industries. In the southern district,
near Lake Huron, are the famous oil springs from which petroleum is obtained. Further to the north are prolific salt wells, the salt obtained from
which forms a large item in the commerce of that neighborhood. The salt
district embraces almost the whole of the County of Huron and considerable portions of Bruce and Lambton. Wells of natural gas have been struck
in various localities between the St. Clair River and the Georgian Bay, in
the Niagara district, at Mimico (near Toronto), and at other places, the gas
being used both for illuminating and manufacturing purposes. There are
also considerable areas of peat beds in several parts of the Province. The
rivers and lakes are well supplied with fish and the forests with game.
But the great and abounding element of Ontario's natural wealth is in its
soil, and to it and its products it is desired to direct the attention of intending emigrants.

Before speaking of the agricultural capabilities of Ontario, it seems
proper to make a brief reference to its government and institutions, so that
the emigrant may form some idea how much, or rather how little of old
world manners and ways that are desirable to preserve, he will have to
part with should he make Ontario his future home. This Province is the
most populous and wealthy in the Dominion. Though the newest of all
the old Provinces, it has made much more rapid progress than any of the
others. Its settlements, extending first along the banks of the St. Lawrence and Ottawa Rivers and the shores of the great lakes, have been grad-
ually pushing backwards towards the north and west, so that now as far
north as and including the County of Renfrew on the east and the County
of Bruce on the west—from the Ottawa River to Lake Huron on a line
about midway between the 45th and 46th parallel—forms one solid and
compact settlement, with Lake Erie, the Niagara River, Lake Ontario
and the River St. Lawrence for its southern boundary. In this are included the whole of the forty-two counties comprising what may be termed

the completely and permanently organized portion of the Province, within which almost all the acquired wealth and nearly the entire population aro concentrated, and in which there is neither a barren spot nor a single township that is not partially occupied. This, though a small part of the territory embraced within the geographical boundaries of the Province (as the reader will perceive by examining the accompanying map) is really what is ordinarily spoken of as "Ontario," but though the county divisions have not yet been pushed further north and west into Muskoka, Parry Sound, Nipissing, Algoma, Thunder Bay and Rainy River Districts (called the unorganized parts of the Province, because County divisions are not yet established) into which the main part geographically speaking of the Province is divided, still the judicial, educational and municipal institutions are carried along with the advance of settlement into these districts, and the inhabitants have also their representatives in the Dominion Parliament and Provincial Legislative Assembly, so that the general institutions of the Province are established in them as in the older localities in so far as they are fitted for their introduction. At the last census, taken in April, 1891, the population of the Province was 2,114,321.

PROVINCIAL AND MUNICIPAL SYSTEMS OF GOVERNMENT.

PROVINCIAL GOVERNMENT.

The Provincial Government has exclusive jurisdiction in questions relating to property and civil rights, education, municipal government, and all other matters of local concern, as distinguished from those of a general character which are under the control of the Dominion or Federal Government at Ottawa. It comprises an Executive, and a Legislative Assembly, forming together what is called the Legislature (or Parliament) for the making, amending or repealing of the laws, having the same powers over the matters assigned to it, and conducting its business with the same forms and under similar rules as the Parliament of Canada, or the Imperial Parliament. The Lieutenant-Governor (representing the Queen, in whose name he sanctions the Bills passed by the Legislative Assembly) is advised by an Executive Council composed of seven members, who form the Cabinet and preside over the seven departments into which the Administration is divided, viz. : Law ; Finance ; Agriculture ; Education ; Public Works ; Crown Lands, and Provincial Secretary. The Ministers hold seats in the Legislative Assembly and administer affairs so long only as they retain the confidence of the people's representatives, precisely after the manner, and following the very forms of British parliamentary government ; but altogether unfettered by any hereditary branch as in Great Britain, or by a nominated senate as in the Dominion. The Legislative Assembly holds annual sessions and is re-elected every four years (unless sooner dissolved) under a manhood suffrage law giving a vote to every man above the age of twenty-one years, who is a British subject by birth or naturalization, and is not a pauper, nor undergoing sentence for crime.

JUDICIAL AND MUNICIPAL SYSTEMS.

The organized portion of the Province (already described) is divided into forty-two counties and these into townships (answering to English or Scotch "parishes," and usually about ten or twelve miles square). The counties have their Judges, Registrars (of Deeds), Sheriffs and County Councils. The County Judge also holds Division (i. e., Small Debt) Courts, in the several Divisions into which his county is divided, several times during the year, and a semi-annual Court of Assize is held at the County Town, so that law and justice in all matters of business or of contention, whether civil or criminal, are brought to the very doors of the people. The County Councils are composed of one or more representatives from each township, town or incorporated village within the geographical limits of the county, and administer all municipal affairs in accordance with the municipal laws of the Province. The townships have also their Councils, whose duty it is to administer local municipal matters, and one or more of whose members represent the township in the County Council. The cities, of which there are eleven, and the towns and villages, of which there are upwards of 200, and the number increasing every year, have also their Municipal Councils, the whole system of municipal government being thoroughly understood and carried out to its fullest extent among the people, nearly all of whom take an active interest in public questions of a local character. The municipal elections are held annually on the first Monday in January, and the electors are composed of the ratepayers, whose names appear on the assessment roll of the previous year.

POWERS OF MUNICIPAL COUNCILS.

The powers and duties of Municipal Councils are defined and regulated by Act of the Legislature, and embrace nearly the whole field of the local administration of public affairs. The levying and collection of taxes for the support of education and the maintenance of public works, including the making and repairing of streets, roads and bridges within the municipality ; the preservation of order, the protection of person and property and the carrying out of sanitary and other regulations for the general well-being of the community ; the borrowing of money for public undertakings ; the supplying of gas, water, etc., are among the principal matters with which the Municipal Councils have to deal within their respective jurisdictions. Township Councils may make and enforce by-laws for the drainage of marsh lands, and for this purpose money is loaned by the Province at a low rate of interest, and repayment is made by a special annual tax levied on the lands thereby benefited. County Councils have jurisdiction in matters common to the whole group of townships, villages and towns embraced within the limits of the County, comprising court houses, gaols and other public buildings, highways, etc., etc. The Local Boards of School Trustees, elected by the people, relieve the municipal councils of the duties incident to the management of the public schools ; and the License Commissioners, appointed by the Government, for the several license districts, which correspond nearly with the parliamentary ridings throughout the Province, control the issuing of hotel, tavern and shop licenses for the sale of liquors,'subject to the Provincial laws in that behalf, and the municipal by-laws made thereunder. The clerks of the several municipalities keep the records of births, marriages and deaths, annual returns of which are made to the government. The returns of the annual assessment or valuation of property made by the assessors (who are appointed by the Councils) furnish the basis upon which the rate of taxation is imposed for the various services of the year. From these returns are also made up the voters' lists, the lists of jurors to serve in the courts, etc. The municipalities have power to establish Houses of Refuge for the destitute, and to grant relief in individual cases of distress ; but Poor Law Guardians and Poor Rates are things unknown in the Province. In the towns and cities charitable institutions of various kinds, sustained mainly by voluntary effort and systematically aided by a small annual grant from the Provincial Exchequer, proportioned to the number of inmates, with a donation more or less liberal from the local municipal funds, amply meet the requirements of public charity, so that the rate-supported " Work-House " has no counterpart among the institutions of Ontario.

EDUCATIONAL INSTITUTIONS, ETC.

The educational institutions of Ontario are such as to place it in the very front rank among the nations of the earth. Not to speak of its higher institutions of learning—its Universities, Colleges and Academies for male and female pupils—it has a Public School system which provides ample means for giving a good common education to all throughout the length and breadth of the land. From the free public school the pupil may graduate to the High School or Collegiate Institute, where he will get an education to qualify him for his University Matriculation Examination. The University of Toronto, a liberally endowed and well appointed institution as now constituted, is, in fact, the complement and completion of the Ontario Educational System, with which are affiliated many of the Ecclesiastical or Denominational Colleges of the Province, while it is purely non-sectarian.

PUBLIC AND SEPARATE SCHOOLS.

The Educational System is administered as a Department of the Government with a member of the Executive Council at its head, and the general management, like that of the Municipal System, is in the hands of the people, through Local Boards of School Trustees elected by the ratepayers. In the rural districts the townships are divided into school sections of convenient size, so that the pupils within the section may be able to attend the school which generally occupies a central position. By this arrangement, and by the additional aid given to "poor sections" in sparsely settled districts, the conveniences of educating the young are carried into the woods with the progress of settlement. The schools are free to the pupils, and attendance either at the public school, or at some private or other school is compulsory between the ages of seven and thirteen years, but the enforcement of the compulsory clause is entirely optional with the authorities in each locality.

The expenditure on Public and Separate School education in 1889 amounted to $4,198,517, while the receipts for the same year were $4,851,061. This money is derived partly from local rates of assessment levied on property, partly from lands originally set apart as Clergy Reserves or for school purposes, and partly from an annual grant from the Legislature. The average cost per pupil at the public schools for 1889, was $8.44.

Separate schools may be established by Roman Catholics in any section or union of sections, and thereupon they receive their own taxes and a proportion of the annual Government grant for the support of such separate school and are released from supporting the public school. Protestants have the like privilege of establishing Protestant separate schools in sections where the teacher of the public school is a Roman Catholic. By these arrangements sectarian strife or wrangling over " mixed " schools is entirely avoided, and both Protestants and Catholics are satisfied. The school law also permits the establishment of separate schools for coloured people, with the same powers and privileges as apply in respect of other separate schools.

The number of persons of school age, that is between five and twenty-one years, in 1889, was 616,028 ; the total number of pupils of all ages attending school was 500,815 ; the total number of teachers was 7,967, and the total number of schools 5,677. These figures include the statistics of the separate schools for Roman Catholics, of which there were 243 in operation in 1889.

MODEL SCHOOLS, ETC.

Another important branch of the system is that of the Model Schools for the training of teachers. They were introduced in 1876, and have since proved most advantageous to the educational progress of the Province, by supplying a class of competently-trained teachers. These schools are distributed throughout the Province to the number of fifty-eight. The number of teachers in training in 1890 was 1,293, and the number passing the final examination, 1,228. Of a higher grade than these are the Training Institutes, authorized in 1885, for the training of Assistant-Masters in High Schools and First-Class Public School Teachers ; and besides these there are several Normal Schools and Collegiate Institutes, all engaged in preparing the youth of both sexes either for a University course, or for the teaching profession, or for any other walk in life they may choose to follow. No other country offers greater, and very few more economical, facilities for obtaining a thorough education ; and this is a consideration which should have great weight with emigrants in deciding where they may cast their lot.

AGRICULTURAL COLLEGE.

The institution known as the Ontario Agricultural College and Experimental Farm, situated about a mile and a quarter from the city of Guelph, forty-nine miles from Toronto, in the midst of a fine farming district, is under the control of the Minister of Agriculture (who is also Commissioner of Immigration and a member of the Executive Council) and was established by the Provincial Legislature, in 1874, for the purpose of giving a thorough knowledge of the theory and practice of farming in all its branches. The main College building is a large and commodious structure, containing students' dormitories, dining-hall, class-rooms, reading-room, library, museum, gymnasium, bath-rooms, etc. ; and near this building is a fine Chemical Laboratory, thoroughly equipped for the most advanced work in agricultural chemistry ; also a large botanical laboratory and a complete set of greenhouses, with all the appliances and conveniences for the most extensive theoretical and practical work in botany and horticulture. The farm consists of 550 acres, 43 of which are still under the original forest. Of the cleared portion, about 333 acres are worked as an ordinary farm, 90 acres devoted to experimental work, and 63 to lawn, garden, etc. The live stock comprises nine breeds of cattle, eight breeds of sheep, several breeds of swine, and a good representation of horses. Every appliance is provided that will aid in imparting a thorough and practical knowledge of agriculture, more especially of those branches which are best adapted for profitable prosecution in the Province, according to conditions of climate and soil. The institution is under the management of a President, with an able staff of Professors, Masters, Instructors and Foremen, all especially qualified for their several departments. The class-room work includes a full and practical course of instruction in (1) Agriculture, Live-stock and Dairying ; (2) Veterinary Science—the structure, diseases, and treatment of farm animals, etc. ; (3) Chemistry, Geology, Botany, Zoology, and the study of insects as to the best means of preventing their ravages ; (4) English Grammar, Composition, Literature, and Political Economy ; (5) Arithmetic, Mensuration, Mechanics, Levelling, and Book-keeping. The students are also required to spend a portion of their time at manual labour, for which purpose they are sent in rotation to the farm, garden, live-stock, carpenter-shop, and experimental department, and are paid for this work at rates varying from four to ten cents per hour. Most of the students reside in the College and are required to pay for board and lodging at the rate of two dollars and a half per week. The fees for tuition are equally moderate, being for residents who are the sons of farmers, or who have served an apprenticeship of one year on a farm, $20 a year ; for residents who are not farmers' sons, and have not served an apprenticeship on a farm, $30 a year ; for non-residents who have served an apprenticeship on a Canadian farm, $50 a year ; and for non-residents who have not served an apprenticeship, $100 for the first, and $50 for the second year.   It will be observed that the scale of fees is graduated in favour of the people of the Province.

This institution has conferred great benefits on the agriculturists of the Province, by the importation of thoroughbred stock from Great Britain, and by holding periodical sales as the animals multiply on the farm.   In order that farmers in all parts of the Province may share equally in the advantages of this arrangement, the animals bought at the sale are delivered at the purchaser's residence free of expense.   It must be obvious that such an institution is calculated to aid very materially in the development of every branch of agricultural industry.   An eminent English authority says of it :—" The students receive an agricultural education in which Science is happily blended with practice, and theory is borne out by demonstration."   The tenant-farmer delegates who visited Canada in 1890 on the invitation of the Dominion Government also speak of it in the most flattering terms.   Mr. William Edwards, of Ruthin, Wales, says :—" The advantages to the young men who attend it are manifold, and the knowledge acquired in the short space of two years is such as to enable them to start at once upon a successful career ; and in whatever part of the earth they may take up their abode, their example will act as a stimulant to their neighbours, and prove of great national value."   Mr. G. Hutchinson, of Brougham Castle, Penrith, Mr. John T. Wood, of The Court, Halewood, and all the other delegates who have mentioned it in their reports, speak of it in the highest terms of commendation.

FARMERS' INSTITUTES.

Under the direction of the President of the College, a series of meetings is held throughout the different counties at stated periods, called " Farmers' Institutes," at which the farmers of the county or neighborhood assemble to exchange experiences and discuss improved methods of prosecuting their calling.   These meetings are attended by one or more of the professors of the College, or by other competent lecturers, who give instructions suitable to the season, and with a view of improving the methods pursued in that particular locality.   Butter making, cheese making, sheep farming, the rearing of young cattle, etc., etc., as well as the varieties of manure, the management of the soil, and kindred subjects, form the ordinary topics of discussion at these " Institutes," and much good has already been effected by them.

TRAVELLING DAIRIES.

Another feature in connection with the Agricuitural College, and one which has excited great interest throughout the Province, is the introduction of Travelling Dairies, three of which are at work in different localities. They are sent out by direction of the Minister of Agriculture, moving from county to county, and at convenient places in each giving practical object lessons in butter making, with lectures on that subject and the proper care of milk and cream, the feeding of cows, etc. The movements of these dairies are under the immediate control of the President of the College.

AGRICULTURAL SOCIETIES, ETC.

The County and Township Agricultural Societies, sustained partly by the Government and partly by voluntary contributions, through the agency of their annual exhibitions stimulate progress by healthful competition and a liberal distribution of prizes. The Bureau of Statistics, established by the Government, for the collection and monthly publication of crop reports, and the official collection and dissemination of statistics, and other information bearing on the condition and progress of agriculture and other industries, furnishes another and a valuable aid to the farmer, in making his calculations as to crops and markets.

The government also makes an allowance from the public chest to assist the farmers in planting shade trees on the highways adjoining their farms, where the local municipalities undertake the superintendence of the work. In so far as legislation can be made to encourage the farmer in carrying enterprises to profitable results, he can have no possible reason of complaint against the Ontario Legislature, but, on the contrary, many good reasons for thankfulness that his interests have been so well considered, and this perhaps may safely be said to have resulted from the large measure of influence which he enjoys in the direction of public affairs.

CHURCHES, NATIONAL SOCIETIES, ETC.

Ontario is most liberally supplied with churches. The principal denominations of Christians rank as to numbers in the following order, as given in the census of 1891 : Methodists (the several bodies of Methodists are united in one as the " Methodist Church of Canada "), 653,942 ; Presbyterians, 453,146 ; Church of England, 385,999 ; Roman Catholics, 358,300 ; Baptists, 105,957. All denominations stand on the same footing before the law, there being no State Church, nor church rates, nor tithes. They are all supported on the voluntary principle, and while apparently having an abundant supply of funds for their own proper purposes, they contribute liberally to charitable and missionary enterprises, both within and without the Dominion of Canada. The feeling prevailing among the several bodies towards each other is one of friendly sympathy and rivalry in doing good, and religious distinctions are entirely excluded from consideration in the combinations which form the two great political parties of Liberals and Conservatives.

National and benevolent societies, temperance societies in connection with, or indepent of, the churches, literary and musical societies, and social clubs, are plentiful in the cities and towns, and there are numerous ways of maintaining social intercourse in the rural districts. Upon the whole the British emigrant who settles down in Ontario, will find that social life there is very much like what it is "at home" among the well-to-do people, both in town and country—except that in Ontario the freedom of intercourse may strike him as being somewhat less restrained. He will mingle with people of the same stock as himself, but he will find a more intimate and friendly admixture of English, Scotch and Irish than he is likely to have been accustomed to before. He will have transferred himself from the land where the three nations make one kingdom, to the land where the children of the three nations make one people ; but in this change, either in its social or its political aspects, he will find nothing that should wound his susceptibilities ; but rather let it be hoped the freer development of the most estimable qualities in each harmonizing in the formation of a new national character, alike honourable to the people of Canada, and to the countries from which they have sprung.

CLIMATE.—FARM WORK OF THE DIFFERENT SEASONS.

The climate of Ontario varies according to latitude, elevation and situation with reference to the great lakes, but is, upon the whole, one of the most pleasant and healthful in the world. The extremes of heat and cold are far greater than in Great Britain, but the purity and dryness of the atmosphere render the hottest days in summer, as well as the coldest in winter, endurable without discomfort. Fogs are rarely seen, except in the mornings of spring and autumn, and though the rainfall averages about the same as that of Great Britain, one year with another, yet the "rainy days" are much fewer in number, and more certain in their seasons of recurrence. The old description of Canadian seasons—"six

2

months of winter and six months of summer"—is not true of any Province in the Dominion, though it may be approximately correct as to some localities in the north-eastern and north-western territories. But as to Ontario it has no application whatever.

In the southern region, bordering on the lower lakes (Erie and Ontario) the winter usually begins about Christmas and lasts until the latter part of March. Further to the north it begins a little earlier, say about the middle of December, and breaks up during the first or second week in April. Except in the northern region there is no winter in Ontario lasting over four months, and its average duration in the settled portion of the Province (previously described) is from three months in the southern and western to three and a-half or at the most four months in the eastern and northern districts. The winter storms are comparatively rare—such violent hurricanes, cyclones, or "blizzards" as occasionally visit the western States of the American Union, carrying death and destruction before them, are altogether unknown—and the public highway and railway traffic is never "blocked," or interrupted, more than a few hours at a time, even in the stormiest weather. Though in the northern part of the Province the winter begins earlier and breaks up later than in the southern, yet so far as settlement has yet advanced to the west and north the seasons have offered no bar to the successful prosecution of agriculture.

April ushers in the spring which comes with great rapidity, the luxuriant vegetation being a perennial source of wonder and admiration even to those who have witnessed it for twenty or thirty years, but whose memories recur to the slower growth with which they were made familiar in the country where they spent their youth. For the practical purposes of the farm the spring is a "short" season and a busy one. The genial rains which fall liberally in April and May, and the increasing warmth of air and soil push forward vegetation with great vigor, and in a few weeks the summer time and the harvest are hurried on together.

The summer season is usually reckoned from the middle or end of May to the middle of September. Under the steady warmth and refreshed by occasional brief but copious showers, the crops make rapid progress, and the month of June is hardly finished ere the hum of preparation for the harvest is heard. Hay-cutting begins about the end of June, and the wheat harvest in the first week of July, in the most southern parts of the Province. In other localities both operations begin a week or two later according to situation. All the other grain crops follow in rapid succession, so that before the end of August the grain harvest is completed throughout the Province. The harvest time is usually the period of extreme summer heat, yet those who work in the open field, under the rays of the sun in the middle of the hottest days, seldom suffer injury or even serious discomfort if they use ordinary precautions for their protection.

The extremes of temperature show a wide range on the thermometer, varying from about 90° Fahr. or upwards, in the hottest days of summer, to 12° or more below zero in the coldest days of winter. The following table shows the average statistics of temperature, sunshine and rainfall of the Province for the six growing months (April—Sept.) in 1891, with the averages of ten years 1882—'91 :

Months.	Temperature.		Sunshine.		Rainfall.	
	1891.	Ten Years.	1891.	Ten Years.	1891.	Ten Years.
	Deg.	Deg.	Hrs.	Hrs.	Ins.	Ins.
April......	42.97	40.22	190.7	190.9	1.77	1.54
May	51.94	52.63	229.6	212.5	1.07	2.63
June	65.43	63.35	245.5	246.2	1.84	2.97
July	63.70	66.79	249.2	270.2	3.50	2.64
August	64.81	64.32	217.3	234.7	3.93	2.69
September.......	61.53	57.76	231.0	195.8	2.03	2.52
Six months ...	58.40	57.51	1363.3	1350.3	14.14	14.99

The autumn season, called the "Fall," is the most deliciously-enjoyable weather of the whole year to those who do not give the preference to the crisp air, the keen frost and the music of the sleigh-bells in winter. Autumn is not less beautiful than summer ; the atmosphere is cooler, but in October, and sometimes in November the days are of a genial warmth, and the nights cool and refreshing. The operations on the farm at this season consist mainly of preparations for the next approaching seasons of winter and spring. The gathering and storing of root crops, the "fall" ploughing and the preparations generally for wintering stock, etc., should keep the farmer and his help busy, whenever the state of the weather permits. It is usual to have a flurry of snow some time in November, which, however, seldom lies more than a day or two, when it disappears, and the cool, open weather, with occasional heavy rains, runs well on through December, especially in the south-western districts.

There is much misconception as to the severity and unbearableness of the extremes of Canadian seasons. But neither the winter, by the rigor

of its cold, nor the summer, by the intensity of its heat, should frighten
away the British emigrant from the Province of Ontario. The testimony
of those who have had experience of the seasons both in Britain and
Ontario, is without exception favourable to the climate of the latter as
being decidedly more salubrious and enjoyable throughout the whole
year. It may be mentioned also that the summer days are shorter and
the winter days are longer in Ontario than in Britain, and with the pure,
dry atmosphere, the bright sunshine of the day-time and the clear star-lit
sky at night, which are common characteristics of a Canadian winter, this
season, besides being one of great commercial activity, offers numerous
facilities for healthful exercise and rational enjoyment, and is welcomed
by many as the most delightful of all the seasons. The snow, it should
be mentioned, instead of being a barrier to travel, as in many other
countries, is the great improver of the roads. In winter sleighs are sub-
stituted for wheeled vehicles, and horses can then draw much heavier
loads at greater speed over the the hard-packed snow, which lies on the
ground in most parts of the Province from the beginning to the end of
the winter season.

ACCESS TO MARKET.

The position of Ontario with respect to its means of access to the
markets of the world, is superior to that of nearly every one of it
competitors in the same line of products, and is surpassed by none. The
wheat-growing, the stock-raising, butter and cheese exporting sections of
the United States, and the great grain fields of the future in the Canadian
and American North-West, are not so well placed towards the British
markets (which rule the prices) as is the Province of Ontario. Its
interior means of transport are ample. At half a dozen different points
its railway system connects with that of the United States. Its magnifi-
cent system of lake, canal and river navigation accommodates not alone
its own trade, but also a great portion of the trade of the Western States.
Its seaports are Montreal and Quebec in summer, and Portland and
Halifax in winter, with access at all times to Boston, New York, etc.,
etc. Toronto, its capital, the seat of the Government and Legislature, of
the Universities and other institutions of learning, and of the Law Courts,

is a fine and flourishing city of 181,220 inhabitants, and offers a ready market for much that the farmer has to sell. It is the headquarters of the principal exporters of live stock and of the leading men in commercial and manufacturing business, and the centre of a complete network of railways extending throughout the Province in all directions. The trip from Toronto to Liverpool can now be made with ease and comfort in nine days, or even less time ; and the British farmer does not require to be told that the rates of freight are such that beef, butter, cheese, etc., can be carried from Ontario, laid down in English markets and sold at prices so low that he cannot profitably compete with them. But he can secure a profitable return for his capital and his skill by transferring both to the Province of Ontario and entering on agricultural pursuits.

The markets throughout the Province are within easy reach of the farmer in every settled district. The highways are substantially made and kept in good repair, the towns and villages are thickly dotted over the country, being seldom more than from five to ten miles apart, and excepting in the new and far northern settlements, almost every farm is within easy reach of a railway station. The question of easy access to market is one which might be supposed to involve serious difficulties in a country embracing such a wide range of distances ; but practically the means of transport are so ample and the freight rates so regulated and upon the whole so low, that there is no settled part of the Province in which it presents material obstacles, either as to cost or convenience.

SOIL, PRODUCTIONS, ETO.

Ontario has many varieties of soil, nearly all of which are fertile and of easy cultivation. The most common are the loams of different kinds, black, clay and sandy. There are also light and heavy clay soils, sandy soils, and in some districts marsh and alluvial soils of great depth resting on clay bottoms. The following eloquent tribute to the excellence of the productions and the capabilities of the soil of Ontario, is from the pen of the Hon. David A. Wells, an eminent American statesman, and is clipped from an article which appeared in the *North American Review*, several years ago. Mr. Wells speaks from an intimate acquaintance with the country on both sides of the International dividing line, and his testimony is valuable as that of one whose knowledge and experience have placed him above the influences of national or sectional prejudices. He says :—

"North of Lakes Erie and Ontario and the River St. Lawrence, east of Lake Huron, south of the 45th parallel, and included mainly within the present Dominion Province of Ontario, there is as fair a country as exists on the North American Continent, nearly as large in area as New York, Pennsylvania and Ohio combined, and equal, if not superior, to these States in its agricultural capacity. It is the natural habitat on this continent of the combing wool sheep, without a full, cheap and reliable supply of the wool of which species the great worsted manufacturing interest of the country cannot prosper, or we should rather say, exist. It is the land where grows the finest of barley, which the brewing interest of the United States must have if it ever expects to rival Great Britain in its present annual export of over $11,000.000 of malt products. It raises and grazes the finest of cattle, with qualities specially desirable to make good the deterioration of stock in other sections, and its climatic conditions, created by an almost encirclement of the Great Lakes, especially fit to grow men. Such a country is one of the greatest gifts of Providence to the human race, better than bonanzas of silver and rivers whose sands contain gold."

The general productiveness of the soil of Ontario, its adaptability for raising all kinds of cereals, and its superiority over every part of the United States in the production of barley, are acknowledged facts. As the seasons vary, however, and the results of the harvest differ very widely, one year from another, it requires a comparison of the same crops extending over a period of several years to give a fair idea of the relative productivenes of the different localities contrasted. With this view the following interesting table, with the compiler's explanatory remarks, is copied from the Eighth Annual Report of the Ontario Bureau of Industries (1890) :

AVERAGE YIELD PER ACRE.

"ONTARIO VS. AMERICAN STATES.—The following table affords an interesting comparison of the average yield per acre in bushels of the principal cereals in Ontario and the best of the grain-growing states of the American Union, the figures being given for 1888 and 1889, together with the averages for the five years 1885-9, and the eight years 1882-9 :

State	Fall Wheat 1889	1888	1885-9	1882-9	Spring Wheat 1889	1888	1885-9	1882-9	Barley 1889	1888	1885-9	1882-9	Oats 1889	1888	1885-9	1882-9
Dakota					9.4	9.7	11.5	13.0	20.3	20.0	20.2	24.8	15.5	27.2	27.3	31.4
California	13.3	12.1	11.5	12.1					20.3	20.0	20.2	19.7	25.0	28.8	27.3	26.9
Nebraska					12.0	9.3	10.7	11.8	22.7	22.5	22.3	22.2	31.6	25.8	29.7	30.7
Kansas	18.4	15.2	13.0	14.9					24.0	20.5	21.4	21.5	31.5	25.3	28.3	30.4
Missouri	13.0	12.0	12.4	11.9					21.0	18.4	20.5	21.0	25.5	25.2	25.1	26.4
Iowa					13.1	9.8	11.3	11.3	22.6	21.0	21.8	21.8	34.5	26.2	31.8	32.6
Minnesota					14.6	9.0	12.1	14.7	25.6	18.5	21.8	22.4	28.0	28.7	31.2	33.1
Wisconsin					14.2	11.5	11.8	12.5	24.5	22.5	32.8	23.3	35.5	29.4	30.3	30.6
Illinois	16.0	13.7	13.4	13.3					21.6	22.4	21.7	22.3	37.5	35.8	33.5	34.6
Indiana	14.7	16.0	12.8	12.9					21.3	18.7	19.3	20.0	27.7	26.5	27.7	28.2
Michigan	14.7	14.6	15.6	15.6					22.4	22.0	22.0	21.6	33.7	33.2	32.3	32.6
Ohio	14.6	13.5	12.7	13.0					21.5	22.4	22.0	22.0	32.3	31.8	32.8	31.6
Pennsylvania	12.3	13.5	11.0	12.3					18.3	18.2	18.2	19.8	26.2	26.5	26.3	27.4
New York	13.8	14.1	15.0	14.7					21.1	21.8	18.2	22.3	24.5	28.1	26.5	28.0
Ontario	15.8	16.7	18.8	19.4	14.3	17.5	13.9	15.6	26.7	26.1	25.8	26.2	33.5	35.4	34.0	35.3

" In studying this table of comparison it should be remembered that Ontario is pitted against those states only in which the cereals named in the table are staple crops. In fall wheat Ontario comes behind Kansas and Illinois in 1889, but in the averages for the series of years it is 3.8

bushels ahead of the highest state.   Minnesota alone leads the Province
in spring wheat for the year, but the averages for the five and eight years
are in favor of Ontario, which exceeds Minnesota, the highest state by .9
bushel per acic.   The Province sweeps the field in barley, the average
yield of 26.7 bushels for the year being 1.1 more than that of the best
state, and this yield is fully maintained in the averages for the series of
years.   Four out of fourteen states surpass Ontario in the average yield
of oats in 1889, but as in the case of the other cereals the Province leads
in the averages for the five and eight years terms.   Briefly stated,
Ontario continues to head the list in the yields of each of the four grains
for the five and eight years periods."

FARM LANDS AND FIELD CROPS.

The following statistical information concerning the farm lands, live
stock and field crops of the Province for the year 1891 is furnished by the
Ontario Bureau of Industries.   It will be observed in comparing the
average yield per acre in 1891 with the average for ten years that for
last 'year there is a considerable excess in all the leading crops.   This is
not to be explained solely by the fact that the year was an exceptionally
favourable one, for though the returns are not to hand at the time of
writing, the prospect for the present year is fully equal to that of last,
and there is good reason to believe that a part, at least, of the excess
noticed is due to the improved methods of farming which are working
their way amongst the cultivators of the soil through the influence of the
Agricultural College, Farmers' Institutes and other stimulating and
educating agencies :—

"AREA OF FARM LANDS.   The municipal returns show that in 1891,
there were 22,535,983 acres of farm lands assessed, of which 946,421
acres are taxed against non-residents.   There were then 11,802,487 acres
of cleared land, leaving 8,376,762 acres in woodland and 2,356,734 acres
in swamp, marsh or waste lands.   Of cleared lands, 187,832 acres were in
orchard and garden, while 2,721,281 acres (23 per cent.) were devoted to
pasture.

"LIVE STOCK.   The number of live stock on hand on July 1, 1891,
was as follows :

Horses: Working horses, 328,736 ; breeding mares, 127,188 ; colts,
stallions, etc., 222,535 ; total, 678,459.

Cattle : Working oxen, 6,716 ; milch cows, 773,234 ; store cattle, over
2 years, 359,318 ; young and other cattle, 839,547 ; total, 1,978,815.

Sheep : Over 1 year, 935 713 ; under 1 year, 758,038 ; total, 1,693,751.

Hogs: Over 1 year, 224,125 ; under 1 year, 932,191 ; total, 1,156,316.

Poultry: Turkeys, 507,907 ; geese, 458,290 ; other fowls, 6,039,893.

Total value of live stock in 1891, $108,721,076, an increase of $4,634,-
450 over the previous year.

The total wool clip amounted to 5,498,141 ℔, and was valued at
$1,066,639.

" FIELD CROPS. The following table gives the area, produce and value at market prices of the principal field crops grown in Ontario in 1891 :

FIELD CROPS.	Acreage 1891.	Acreage Ten Years.	Product in 1891.	Average Yield per acre 1891.	Average Yield per acre Ten Years.	Value of crop of 1891.	Market price 1891.	Market price Ten Years.
			Bushels.	Bush.	Bush.	$	cts.	cts.
Fall Wheat	849,956	902,846	21,872,488	25.7	20.0	20,800,736	95.1	90.0
Spring Wheat	510,634	563,547	10,711,538	21.0	15.8	9,951,019	92.9	89.6
Barley	553,166	743,245	16,141,904	29.2	26.0	7,925,675	49.1	54.5
Oats	1,840,636	1,663,205	75,009,542	40.8	35.1	27,378,483	36.5	36.0
Rye	67,865	103,636	1,134,630	16.7	16.2	820,337	72.3	60.0
Peas	752,453	668,962	18,323,459	24.4	20.8	11,690,367	63.8	61.6
Corn (in the ear)	241,086	195,878	18,288,659	75.9	66.1	5,687,773	31.3	29.1
Buckwheat	107,879	69,230	2,608,142	24.2	22.6	1,150,191	44.1	41.8
Beans	41,451	26,201	769,600	18.6	19.9	816,546	106.1	106.8
Potatoes	160,218	155,449	24,055,886	150	121	7,842,219	32.6	41.1
Mangel-wurzels	22,961	19,546	11,779,448	513	437			
Carrots	9,858	10,423	3,814,016	387	351	476,752	28.9	26.8
Turnips	126,075	104,943	68,853,452	546	410	6,885,345	21.2	21.2
Hay and Clover	2,549,975	2,290,495	Tons. 2,392,798	Tons. 0.94	Tons. 1.35	28,498,224	$ c. 11.91	$ c. 10.59
Total	7,834,213	7,517,606				129,923,667		

" These crops occupy 66½ per cent. of the cleared land, pasture 23 per cent. and orchard and garden 1½ per cent., leaving 9 per cent. or a little over 100,000 acres of cleared lands for small crops, barnyard, fallow, etc. All the crops have been valued at the average market quotations with the exception of carrots and turnips, in which cases the prices quoted are evidently for garden produce in small lots. Leaving out mangels, which have not been valued, the average value per acre of the above crops was $16.63 as compared with $16.01 for ten years."

PERMANENT EXHIBIT.

At the exhibition rooms of the Imperial Institute, Imperial Institute Road, Kensington, London, S.W., visitors will find a permanent exhibit of the mineral and other products of Ontario, an examination of which will greatly assist them in forming an accurate judgment as to the productions and resources of the Province.

FLAX CULTURE

Flax culture has been successfully carried on for several years in many parts of the Province, especially in the counties of Wellington, Waterloo, Perth and Oxford. There are about forty flax mills in operation throughout the Province, mostly in the counties named, at some of which a large business is done. The fibre is rendered into rope, binding and other twines, yarn and thread, and the seed into oil and oil cake, for all of which there is ready sale. For the cultivation of flax a friable soil with clay subsoil is very suitable. The land should be free from weeds and from five to six pecks of seed should be sown to the acre. Some of the millers agree with the cultivators to furnish the seed and to buy the crop at a specified price, usually about twelve dollars per ton, and as two tons per acre is about an average crop, that price pays for the whole cost of cultivating and harvesting and leaves a handsome margin for profit. In 1891 the Province exported flax to the value of $181,386.

STOCK RAISING.

Mixed farming prevails generally throughout the Province and is considered the most profitable, though in certain districts special branches are followed with great advantage, and among these, stock-raising deservedly holds high rank. The steady demand in the British markets has imparted to it a stability that renders it one of the most reliable sources of profit to the farmer, while at the same time it serves to maintain and even increase the fertility of the soil. There are many excellent stock farms in Ontario, some of which were visited and very highly commended by the British farmer delegates. But it is more as an important feature n a system of mixed farming than as a specialty, that the attention of the intending immigrant is here directed towards it. His experience as a

British farmer specially qualifies him for successfully prosecuting this system, while the conditions under which agriculture can be most profitably followed in Ontario are particularly favourable to stock-raising and fattening, and the growth of the various rotations of crops after the English and Scotch models. The following compilation from the Dominion Trade and Navigation Tables shows the number and value of the horses, cattle and sheep exported from Canada during the past ten years :—

YEAR.	Horses.		Cattle.		Sheep.		Total Value.
	Number.	Value.	Number.	Value.	Number.	Value.	
		$		$		$	$
1882..	20,920	2,326,637	62,106	2,256,330	311,669	1,228,957	5,811,924
1883..	13,019	1,633,291	66,396	3,898,028	308,474	1,388,056	6,919,375
1884..	11,595	1,617,829	89,263	5,681,082	304,403	1,544,005	8.842,916
1885..	12,310	1,640,506	144,441	7,508,043	335,207	1,264,811	10,413,360
1886..	16,951	2,232,623	92,661	5,916,551	359,488	1,184,106	9,333,280
1387..	19,081	2,350,926	116,490	6,521,320	443,628	1,595,340	10,467,586
1888:.	20,505	2,563,407	100,748	5,012,788	395,320	1,283,537	8,859,732
1889..	17,874	2,226,892	102,980	5,714,526	360,939	1,276,918	9,218,336
1890..	16,709	2,007,533	81,478	6,952,185	316,013	1,276,999	10,236,717
1891..	11,868	1,572,564	117,765	8,774,769	299,587	1,150,865	11,498,198

The total value of the horses, cattle and sheep exported in 1875, was $1,921,755 ; in 1880, it had reached $5,067,646. During the past ten years, notwithstanding considerable fluctuations, the foregoing figures prove that the trade, especially in cattle, has made solid and substantial progress.

DAIRY FARMING.

According to a trustworthy authority, the Canadian dairy farmer has several important advantages over his English contemporary. He can at moderate cost grow very large crops of forage for winter use ; abundant crops of swedes, mangels, carrots and the like can be raised, and clovers and timothy flourish on most soils. These with an abundant supply of water furnish the prime requisites for successful dairy farming. The use of the silo for the preservation of green crops for winter feed has proved of inestimable advantage, and there is a steady market for the product of the dairy, whether in the shape of milk or transformed into cheese or butter, at prices that are fairly remunerative. To those who understand this branch of agricultural industry, Ontario offers a most inviting field as, if managed with ordinary care and intelligence, a dairy farm is a safe investment and a sure source of profit.

CHEESE.

A great impetus was given to dairy farming by the introduction of the factory system for cheese making, the first cheese factory in the Province having been established about twenty-five years ago, by the Hon. Thomas Ballantyne, (now Speaker of the Legislative Assembly) at Black Creek, near Stratford, in the County of Perth. His enterprise proved eminently successful; the system has since been widely extended, and the cheese trade has steadily grown until it is now one of the most important in the Province. Some of the factories are run on individual account though most of them are conducted on the mutual or co-operative plan by companies duly organized, and under the care of an experienced manager who is paid for his services by a percentage on the quantity of cheese manufactured. The supply of milk is drawn from the farms in the surrounding district, generally embracing a radius of three or four miles from the centre at which the factory is situated. Where the factory is managed on the co-operative plan each farmer receives a share of the net proceeds from the sale of the cheese in proportion to the quantity of milk supplied by him to the factory, and his receipts are usually equivalent to an average of from 7½ to 8 cents per gallon. The cheese finds ready sale at the factory at rates varying from 8 to 10 cents per pound, according to the excellence of the article, and the state of the market. The factories are worked only seven months in the year, from April to October inclusive; but during the other five months the dairyman finds ample compensation in the considerable advance which then takes place in the price of both milk and butter to supply the local demand.

Canadian cheese has an established reputation in the English and other outside markets. The importance of the trade may be judged from the fact that during the four years, 1888-91, the value of the quantity exported amounted to $40,118,282, being $1,305,299 more than the total value of the horses, cattle and sheep exported during the same period. The steady growth of the trade is shown by the following statement of the quantities and values exported from Canada during the ten years ending June 30th,

1890, contrasting there with the exports from the United States for the same period :—

EXPORTS OF CHEESE (DOMESTIC MANUFACTURE).

	From Canada.			From United States.		
	Amount, lbs.	Value.	Per pound	Amount, lbs.	Value.	Per pound
		$	cts.		$	cts.
1881	49,255,523	5,510,443	11.2	147,995,614	16,380,248	11.1
1882	50,807,049	5,500,868	10.8	127,989,782	14,058,975	11.0
1883	58,041,387	6,451,870	11.1	99,220,467	11,134,526	11.2
1884	69,755,423	7,251,989	10.4	112,869,575	11,663,713	10.3
1885	79,655,367	8,265,240	10.4	111,992,900	10,444,409	9.3
1886	78,112,927	6,754,626	8.7	91,877,235	7,662,145	8.3
1887	73,604,448	7,108,978	9.7	81,255,994	7,594,633	9.3
1888	84,173,267	8,928,242	10.6	88,008,458	8,736,304	9.9
1889	88,534,837	3,915,684	10.1	84,999,828	7,889,671	9.3
1890	94,260,187	9,372,212	9.9	95,376,053	8,591,042	9.0

In 1891 Canada exported 106,202,140 lbs., of the value of $9,508,800 ; the value of the United States export for the same year was $7,405,376.

There were 838 cheese factories in operation in the Province in 1891. They were supplied by 45,066 patrons with 865 453,574 pounds of milk from 296,196 cows. They made 81,929,042 pounds of cheese, which was sold for $7,656,484, being an average value of $25.85 for the product of each cow. Their total output for 1891 was 13,000,000 pounds more than the average for the previous nine years. During the same period the number of factories has been doubled.

BUTTER.

The butter trade is in a somewhat backward condition considering the many opportunities for its profitable development. In 1891 there were thirty-nine public creameries or butter factories in operation throughout the Province. Returns of the season's business were made by thirty of these to the Bureau of Industries, which showed a total production of 1,402,809 pounds of the value of $287,559. The process of making butter is still, however, mainly confined to the farm, and for the purpose of disseminating correct knowledge and introducing approved methods of carrying it on, the "Travelling Dairies" already mentioned visit the different sections of the Province, showing the process in actual operation, distributing printed instructions, and giving lectures to those who attend the meetings. By these efforts, and by the introduction of improved machinery

into the creameries, the trade will no doubt soon be greatly increased.
The export from Canada in 1890 amounted to 3,189,083 pounds, valued
at $526,654, and in 1891 to 3,964,844 pounds, valued at $624,640. At
most seasons of the year, however, the prices in the home market generally
rule high enough to make butter the most remunerative product of the
dairyman's industry.

FRUIT FARMING.

Fruit farming (embracing vine culture) is another branch to which the
attention of the intending settler should be directed, for Ontario is admirably adapted to this industry, having as Mr. Pitt the English farmer-
delegate says, three essential conditions for perfect apple raising—" late
spring, hot summer and short antumn, wherein the sap stops rising very
soon after the fruit is ripe." Thrifty orchards are laid out on almost every
well managed farm, and in the older settlements their products constitute
in many instances a not unimportant factor among the minor sources of
the farmers' income.   The apple trade has now grown to considerable pro-
portions, and peaches, plums, pears and small fruits find ready sale in the
local markets at remunerative prices.   Apples and all the hardier fruits
can be profitably grown in any part of the Province, but fruit farming has
not been followed to any great extent, except in the Southern region,
which is specially adapted to the purpose.   This region may be roughly
described as extending from Lake Huron along Lakes St. Clair and Erie
to the Niagara River, and including the counties bordering on the western
portion of Lake Ontario.   Professor Sheldon says of it :—

" This portion of Ontario may be regarded as the garden of the Dominion
—literally as well as figuratively the garden—for it is there that apples,
pears, grapes, peaches, melons and the like grow in the greatest profusion,
and with the least trouble on the part of the farmer.   Every farm has an
orchard, and it is purely the farmer's fault if the orchard is not an excellent one, for the climate and the soil are clearly all that can be desired,
and the trees will do their share of the work provided the right sorts are
planted.   It is usual to plant out peach and apple trees alternately and in
rows in a new orchard, and the apple trees are at a distance apart which
will be right when they are full grown ; this is done because the peach
trees come to maturity first, and have done bearing before the apple trees
require all the room ; the peach trees are then cut down and the apple
trees occupy all the room.   These trees are planted in rows at right angles,
so that there is a clear passage between them whichever way we look, and
the land can be freely cultivated among them ; it is, in fact, usual to take
crops of wheat or oats, or maize, from the land during the time the trees
are young, and we often see fine crops of golden grain overtopped by noble
young trees laden with fruit.   A farmer may not, of course, look to fruit

alone to grow rich on, but he often nets a nice roll of dollars out of it, and to say the least, it is conducive to happiness to be well supplied with fruit, while to live in a climate and on a soil that will produce it abundantly is always desirable."

Vineries, orchards and fruit gardens on a large scale are numerous in the Niagara district and westward on the same line till the County of Essex is reached, which is regarded as especially adapted for the profitable cultivation of the vine. M. Girardot, a native of the best wine district of Eastern France, contrasting it with his own country, says :—"The yield here is at least four or five tons to the acre ; there, not more than two. The wines made here are equal to any in Eastern France. From twenty acres of grapes the yield of wine has averaged about 6,000 gallons, and is very remunerative, a profit of $800 (£160) per acre being frequently obtained." In the district of country here referred to, several semi-tropical fruits are brought to perfection. The apricot, nectarine and quince are easily cultivated over an area of several thousand square miles. At Niagara the almond grows out of doors, and the fig is successfully cultivated with scarcely any protection in winter, and ripens two crops in the year. Sorghum, or Chinese sugar cane, grows very well in the southern counties of the Province. Hundreds of acres are planted with this crop, and the variety known as Early Amber is said to yield as much as 300 gallons of syrup per acre.

The Trade and Navigation Tables show the following exports of fruit for the years 1890 and 1891 :—

	Quantity.		Value.	
	1890	1891	1890	1891
			$	$
Apples, (barrels)........	378,475	451,197	993,163	1,390,436
" Dried, (pounds).	91,962	800,650	4,980	49,029
Other fruits	....	....	100,949	221,795
			1,099,092	1,661,260

Increase in value, 1891, over previous year, $562,168.

THE TIMBER TRADE.

The timber trade, or as it is called in Canada, the "lumber" trade, offers a safe and profitable field for the employment of capital under experienced management. A considerable portion of the Province is still under the original forest and for a long time to come this trade will continue to be one of Ontario's chief industries. It supplies a near and convenient market for certain bulky farm products, and gives employment to a class who go to the "shanties," that is, work in the woods, during the winter months and hire out as farm labourers for the rest of the year. Those farm labourers who are also good axemen, or who take a share of work at the lumber camp have thus an opportunity of commanding the highest rate of wages throughout the whole year, for during the winter months when wages on the farm are at the lowest rate they are at the highest among the men employed in lumbering operations.

THE MINING INDUSTRY.

The rapid increase in the number and importance of mining enterprises and the many fresh discoveries of rich mineral deposits within recent years, induced the government to establish, in connection with the Department of Crown Lands, a Bureau of Mines with a director as chief officer, for the general administration of affairs connected with the mining interests of the Province ; and in 1892 the laws relating to mining and mineral lands were consolidated in one Act entitled "The Mines Act, 1892." In accordance with its provisions, any person may explore for mines or minerals on unoccupied Crown lands, whether surveyed or unsurveyed, and these lands may be acquired from the Crown as surveyed locations, or, if situated within a mining division, may be occupied and worked as staked claims under license, the fee for which is $5 per year. Parties holding separate licenses may form a partnership and work together, or single holders of a license may employ one or more assistants, but a license holder cannot work a claim by the agency of another person. A mining division is a tract set apart by the Government under the superintendence of an inspector, who, acting under the Director of the Bureau of Mines, sees to the enforcement of the Mining Act and the regulations made thereunder. Locations range from 40 to 320 acres, and claims from 10 to 20 acres on vein or lode. Locations situated north of French River are sold at \$2.50 to \$3.50 per acre, and south of it at \$2 to \$2.50 according to the distance from railway accommodation. But, if preferred, the locations may be taken up under leasehold for a period of twenty years, renewable, in which case the rental for land north of French river is \$1 per acre for the first year and 25 cents for subsequent years, and for land south of that river, 60 cents for the first year and 15 cents for subsequent years. Should the holder at any time desire to convert his title into a freehold, the first year's rental will apply on the purchase money. A minimum amount of development work is required to be done within seven years of the issuing of the patent or lease. Claims must be worked continuously, and the yearly rental is one dollar per acre. The Act imposes a royalty on certain specified ores of 2 to 3 per cent. on the value of the ore at the pit's mouth, less the cost of labour and explosives, but this is not to be exacted until seven (or in the case of an original discovery, fifteen) years after the date of the patent or lease.

The report of the Bureau of Mines for 1891 says :—

"Important discoveries are being made every year, and no doubt much of our wealth yet lies hidden in the earth. The deposits of iron ore on the Atik-Okan and Mattawan rivers, which are believed to be of vast extent, have for the most part been discovered within the last two years. The nickel ores of the Sudbury district were unknown six years ago, and during the past year many large and rich finds have been made. Promising gold leads have been found at various points between the Thessalon river and Temagami lake, as well as in the county of Hastings. Extensive beds of kaolin are now known to exist on the eastern and western tributaries of the Moose river, the Abittibi and Missinaibi, valuable for the manufacture of fine pottery, and perhaps more valuable still for the production of aluminum, a semi-noble metal that seems likely to become almost as useful in the arts as iron itself. Then it is only four years ago that we became conscious of having a clay suitable for the manufacture of pressed brick and architectural terra-cotta of the very best quality, and we know now, what was not suspected at first, that a bed of it in the Medina formation is 400 to 600 feet in depth and lies exposed for more than a hundred miles within easy reach of the principal cities of the province."

The same report has the following table of the mineral statistics of the province for the year 1891, shewing (1) the product, (2) the number of mines or works, (3) the quantity produced and (4) the value of the product :—

1. Product.	2 No.	3 Quantity.		4 Value.
				$
Building stone........	84			1,000,000
Cement	5	bbl.	48,211	44,501
Lime..........	130	bush.	2,350,000	300,000
Common brick........	250	no.	160,000,000	950,000
Pressed brick, roofing tile and terra-cotta	7	no.	13,617,909	156,699
Drain tile	60	no.	7,500,000	90,000
Sewer tile..................	3	no.	1,375,000	270,000
Pottery	30			45,000
Gypsum	6	ton	5,350	12,200
Phosphate.................	11	ton	4,900	50,800
Salt........................	17	ton	44,167	157,000
Mica	4	ton	240	31,200
Nickel	8	ton	85,790	324,240
Silver	4	ton	14,925	64,475
Petroleum, crude..........		bbl.	894,647	1,209,558
Total value of mineral productions for the year.................				$4,705,673

Throughout nearly the whole of the mineral region there are tracts of more or less extent that are well adapted for agricultural purposes. The proximity of mining operations affords the advantage of a local market, as well as opportunity for occasional employment to the settlers, so that farming in these localities will become prosperous in proportion to the development of mining enterprise.

PRICE OF FARM LANDS.

To those having the means and the inclination to purchase, there are no difficulties in the way of obtaining farms in any part of the Province, as for one reason or another there are always to be found owners who are willing to sell. The following remarks concerning the selling price and the average value of farms are merely designed to give intending purchasers a general idea of the current rates prevailing, for it will be readily understood that one farm might be very dear at the average rate obtaining in its neighbourhood, while the one adjoining might be an excellent bargain at a much higher figure.

The price of farming land varies much according to locality. In the neighbourhood of the cities and large towns in the old settled districts it ranges from $75 to $100 (£15 to £20 sterling) per acre, exclusive of the value of the buildings, and from these figures it runs all the way down to $2 (eight shillings sterling) per acre for partially cleared farms in the newly settled districts in the northern and north-eastern part of the Province. But in speaking of the price of a farm in Ontario, it is usually rated at so much per acre, including buildings, fencing, and all fixed improvements ; hence many of the so-called highly-priced farms may carry a charge of twenty dollars or more per acre on account of the value of the dwelling house, stables, barns and other outbuildings, which are sometimes very commodious, substantial structures of brick or stone, costing from $2,000 to $5,000, or more.

The price for good farms in the best agricultural districts in the old settlements, away from close proximity to the cities, ranges from $40 to $75 (£8 to £15) per acre, and at this figure usually a large amount of the purchase money may remain unpaid for a term of years, secured by mortgage at a rate of interest not exceeding six per cent. In the newer counties, where the land is but partially cleared, where a half or three-fourths of the farm is still in its primitive wooded condition, or "in bush," as the local phrase has it, prices range from $10 to $40 (say £2 to £8) per acre for really good farms, in good situations, to still lower figures where the situation and soil are not so favourable.

The *average* value of farm land and farm buildings throughout the entire Province, as shewn by the returns for 1890 to the Bureau of Industries, is $27.79 per acre for land and $8.63 per acre for buildings, or a total of $36.42 per acre. As shewn by the same returns, the following counties give the four highest and the four lowest

AVERAGE VALUES PER ACRE :—

COUNTIES.	Land.	Buildings.	Total.
	$ c.	$ c.	$ c.
York...	59 73	17 04	76 77
Wentworth	49 83	17 17	67 00
Brant	47 46	17 76	65 22
Oxford	47 41	15 55	62 96
Haliburton	1 77	0 48	2 25
Renfrew	8 18	2 76	10 94
Frontenac	12 51	4 45	16 96
Lanark	14 50	5 20	19 70

The average value in the Districts of Muskoka, Parry Sound, Nipissing and Algoma is $3.73 per acre for land and $1.02 per acre for farm buildings ; total, $4.75 per acre.

In this region of cheap farms, which lies immediately north of the oldest-settled portions of the Province, and between the Ottawa river and the Georgian Bay, stock-raising and sheep-farming might be followed with profit, as the land is exceptionally well watered, produces abundant root crops and is admirably fitted for grazing purposes. Here a large area of land might be acquired for a less sum than would purchase a hundred acre farm on the frontier, while ordinary skill in the branches of agricultural industry just indicated could not fail to secure a handsome return.

RENTED FARMS.

It is generally sound policy for an immigrant, even if he has the means to buy a farm when he lands in the Province, to put himself in the way of acquiring some experience of the country before he makes a purchase. This may be done in two ways : (1) If disposed to undertake the manual labour of the farm he can hire out for a season or two, or (2) should he deem that course unsuitable he can readily rent a farm for a short term of years, one, two or three years' leases being not uncommon, at a moderate rental of from $2 to $4 per acre, payable in money, or for a certain portion of the crop, etc., (say one-third) in kind. The latter arrangement is not recommended to a stranger ; it is better for him to make his bargain for so much cash. In renting farms it is usual only to calculate the rental on the number of cleared acres. The returns for 1890 show a fraction over twelve per cent. of the farming land of the Province under lease at an average rental of $2.72 per acre of cleared land.

LANDS FOR SALE TO ACTUAL SETTLERS.

In the Algoma and Nipissing districts there are a number of townships in which the government lands are open for sale at the rate of twenty cents (about nine pence halfpenny sterling) per acre, subject to the following conditions ;—Actual residence for three years from the date of purchase ; clearing and having under cultivation at least ten acres for every one hundred acres purchased ; and building a habitable house at least sixteen by twenty feet. The pine trees are reserved until the 30th

April after the issue of the patent. Agencies for the sale of these lands are established at Thessalon and Spanish River. Subject to the same conditions, except that the residence must be for four years, the agencies at Sudbury and Sturgeon's Falls, on the Canadian Pacific Railway, have government lands for sale in the adjoining townships at the rate of fifty cents (two shillings sterling) per acre, one-half payable at the date of purchase and the balance in two years, with interest at the rate of six per cent.

RAILWAY LANDS.

At the session of the Legislature in 1839 an Act was passed, granting Government aid for the construction of certain railways through the northern districts, and for the purpose of forming a fund to recoup the Province for the moneys thus expended, it was provided that a tract of land at least ten miles in width on each side of the lines of railway should be set apart and sold at a rate of not less than two dollars per acre. In accordance with this provision, many townships and parts of townships, formerly classed in the Free Grant list have been withdrawn therefrom in consequence of their being situated within the ten mile belts mentioned, and placed on the list of "Railway Lands," which are open for sale at the rate of two dollars per acre on the following terms and conditions : When such lands possess a mineral value they will be sold at $2 per acre cash under the Mining Act, and the patent will be issued at once ; and when suitable for agricultural purposes, they will be sold at $2 per acre payable one-third cash, and the balance in two equal annual instalments, with interest at six per cent. The purchaser will be entitled to a patent at the expiration of two years from the date of sale upon completion of settlement duties, viz.: two years actual occupation, clearing and having under crop ten acres for every hundred acres, and the erection of a habitable house 16x20. The pine timber is reserved except what may be necessary to the purchaser for building and fencing. The agents for the Free Grant Lands are also agents for the sale of the railway lands. (See list of agencies page 39.)

FREE GRANT LANDS.

Immigrants are not advised to go into the free grant townships with the view of taking up land until they have first had some practical experience of the ways of the country. But many have done so with

success, and those who are disposed to adopt that course would do wel
to give themselves ample time [and opportunity to explore the land and
make their selection of a location in the summer or early part of the
autumn, the latter season being the most favorable for commencing
operations on a bush farm. Since the opening to settlement of the free
grant lands, there have been 9,947 patents issued to actual settlers, an
average of about 525 a year since 1873, when the first issue tock place.

There are now one hundred and fifty-four townships open for location
under the "Free Grant and Homesteads Act of 1868," each containing
from 50,000 to 60,000 acres. Other townships will be opened as railways
and colonization roads are constructed. There are twenty-one local agencies
established throughout the free grant districts, each agent having a
specified number of townships assigned him.

The following is a summary of the regulations respecting Free Grants:—
The Lieutenant-Governor in Council is authorized to appropriate lands,
not being mineral lands or pine timber lands, as free grants to actual
settlers, under regulations to be made for that purpose ; no such grant to
be made to a male under eighteen, or for more than 200 acres. The
patent (or deed from the Crown) is issued to the settler at the expiration
of five years after the taking up of the land, provided the settlement
duties have been performed ; and failure to perform the settlement duties
forfeits the location. The head of a family, whether male or female,
having children under eighteen years of age, can obtain a grant of 200
acres, and a single man over eighteen years of age, or a married man having no children under eighteen residing with him, can obtain a grant of
100 acres in the Free Grant Districts.

Any locatee under the Act, being the head of a family as aforesaid, is
allowed to purchase an additional 100 acres at 50 cents per acre, cash, at
the time of such location, subject to the same reservations and conditions
and the performance of the same settlement duties as are provided in
respect of Free Grant locations, except that actual residence and building
on land purchased will not be required.

The settlement duties are : —To have fifteen acres on each grant
cleared and under crop, of which at least two acres are to be cleared and
cultivated annually for five years ; to build a habitable house, at least
16x20 feet in size ; and to reside on the land at least six months in each
year.

FREE GRANT AGENCIES.

The following is a list of the Free Grant Agencies, with the names of the townships attached to each, and directions for reaching the offices of the several agents :

1. MUSKOKA :—Contains twenty townships, viz. :—Baxter, Brunel, Chaffey, Draper, Franklin, Macaulay, Medora, Monck, Morrison, Muskoka, McLean, Oakley, Ridout, Ryde, Sinclair, Sherborne, Stephenson, Stisted, Watt and Wood. Agent, Wm. Kirk, Bracebridge. The route from Toronto to Bracebridge is by the Northern, and the Northern and Pacific Junction Railways, and the ports on Lakes Muskoka, Rosseau and Joseph, by steamer in summer and by stage in winter.

2. PARRY SOUND :—Contains ten townships, viz. :—Cardwell, Carling, Ferguson, Hagerman, Humphrey, McConkey, McKenzie, McKellar, Shawanaga and Wilson. Agent, Mrs. Theresa Mackay, Parry Sound. In summer, the best route is from Toronto to Penetanguishene or Midland, by the Northern or Midland Railways, and thence to Parry Sound by steamer. In winter, from Toronto to Utterson by the Northern Railway, and thence by stage to Parry Sound, a distance of 48 miles.

3. MAGNETAWAN :—Contains ten townships, viz. :—Chapman, Croft,. Ferrie, Gurd, Lount, Machar, Mills, Pringle, Spence and Strong. S. G. Best, Agent, Magnetawan, township of Chapman. The route is from Toronto to Burk's Falls by railway, in summer, from there to Magnetawan, 20 miles, by steamer. In winter. from Burk's Falls to Magnetawan by stage, 14 miles.

4. EAST PARRY SOUND :—Contains five townships, viz. :—Armour,. Bethune, Joly, Perry and Proudfoot. Edward Handy, Agent, Emsdale, township of Perry. The route is by railway from Toronto, Emsdale being a station on the Northern and Pacific Junction Railway.

5. NIPISSING :—Contains five townships, viz. :—Hardy, Himsworth, Laurier, Nipissing and Patterson. John S. Scarlett, Agent, Powassan. The route from Toronto is by Northern Railway to Powassan. From the east by the Canadian Pacific Railway to Callender, thence by the Northern Railway to Powassan.

6. MATTAWAN :—Contains five townships, viz. : — Calvin, Ferris, Bonfield, Mattawa and Papineau. B. I. Gilligan, Agent, Mattawa. The route is by the Northern and Pacific Junction Railway, or the Canadian Pacific Railway.

7. MINDEN :—Contains seven townships, viz.:—Anson, Glamorgan, Hindon, Lutterworth, Minden, Stanhope and Snowdon. Wm. Fielding, Agent, Minden. The route is from Whitby or Port Hope to Minden Station by the Midland Railway, thence to Minden by stage ; or from Toronto to Coboconk by railway, and from Coboconk to Minden by stage.

. HALIBURTON :—Contains five townships, viz.:—Cavendish, Galway, Bangor, McClure and Wicklow. Chas. R. Stewart, Agent, Haliburton. The route is from Toronto or Port Hope by railway to Haliburton.

9. PETERBOROUGH OR BURLEIGH ROAD :—Contains four townships, viz.:—Anstruther, Chandos, Cardiff and Monmouth. D. Anderson, Agent, Apsley, township of Anstruther. The route is from Toronto or Port Hope to Lakefield by railway, and thence to Apsley by stage.

10. NORTH HASTINGS :—Contains nine townships, viz.:—Carlow, Cashel, Dungannon, Faraday, Herschel, Limerick, Mayo, Monteagle and Wollaston. J. R. Tait, Agent, L'Amable, township of Dungannon, The route from Trenton is by the Central Ontario Railway to Rathbun Station, thence to L'Amable by stage, a distance of eleven miles.

11. FRONTENAC AND ADDINGTON :—Contains nine townships. viz.:—Abinger, Ashby, Effingham, Canonto North, Canonto South, Clarendon, Denbigh, Miller and Palmerston. G. W. Dawson, Agent, Plevna, township of Clarendon. The route is from Kingston by the Kingston and Pembroke Railway, and by stage. [Townships in this agency withdrawn from Free Grant List and open for sale as "Railway Lands." See page 37.]

12. RENFREW, NORTH :—Contains nine townships, viz. :—Alice, Buchanan, Fraser, Head, Maria, McKay, Petewawa, Rolph and Wylie. J. Stewart, Agent, Pembroke. The route is by Canadian Pacific Railway.

13. RENFREW, CENTRE :—Contains three townships of Free Grant and six of Railway Lands. James Reeve, Agent, Eganville, township of Grattan. The route is from Brockville to Cobden by Canadian Pacific Railway, and thence to Eganville by stage.

14. RENFREW, SOUTH :—Contains eight townships, viz.:—Brougham, Brudenell, Griffith, Lyndoch, Matawatchan, Radcliffe, Raglan and Sebastopol. John Whelan, Agent, Brudenell. The route is by Canadian Pacific Railway to Cobden, and thence by stage. [Withdrawn from Free Grant List and open for sale as " Railway Lands." See page 37.]

15. BRUCE MINES :—Contains one township, viz.:—Plummer. Wm. L. Nichols, Agent, Thessalon. The route is from Toronto to Collingwood or Owen Sound by railway, and thence by steamer to Bruce Mines,

and in winter by the Northern and Pacific Junction Railway to North Bay, and thence by the Algoma Branch of the Canadian Pacific Railway to Bruce Mines.

16. St. Joseph Island :—Contains the township of St. Joseph Island. Agent, George Hamilton, Richard's Landing. The route is the same as to Bruce Mines.

17. Sault Ste. Marie :—Contains three townships, viz.:—Korah, Parke and Prince. William Turner, Agent, Sault Ste. Marie. The route from Toronto is by railway to Collingwood or Owen Sound, and thence by steamer ; in winter, by the Northern and C. P. Railways to Sault Ste. Marie.

18. Thunder Bay :—Contains two Free Grant and eleven Railway Lands townships. J. F. Ruttan, Agent, Port Arthur, The route is by railway to Collingwood or Owen Sound, and thence by steamer to Port Arthur, or by railway direct from Toronto to Port Arthur.

Rainy River Agencies.

. T. J. F. Marsh, Rainy River P.O., Agent for the townships of Roseberry, Shenston, Tait, Pattullo, Morley, Dilke, Nelles, Blue, Worthington, Curran and Atwood.

20. Wm. Wilson, Fort Francis P.O., Agent for the townships of Barwick, Lash, Aylsworth, Devlin, Woodyatt, Crozier, Roddick and McIrvine.

21. Archibald Campbell, Rat Portage, who will furnish intending settlers with the number of lots open for location, as well as valuable general information regarding the district.

RAINY RIVER DISTRICT.

By an Act passed at the session of the Legislature, held in 1886, the Free Grant system is extended to the Rainy River District upon the same terms and conditions of settlement as above set forth, excepting that in the Rainy River District the patent is issued after three years, instead of five. The quantity of land which may be obtained is one hundred and sixty acres to a head of a family having children under eighteen years of age residing with him (or her) ; and one hundred and twenty acres to a single man over eighteen, or to a married man not having children under eighteen residing with him ; each person obtaining a free grant to have the privilege of purchasing forty acres additional at the rate of one dollar per acre, payable in four annual instalments. Several townships have already been surveyed on the Canadian bank of the Rainy River on the one mile square section plan—the same as has been followed in the North-West. The Ontario Legislature has adopted and legalized these surveys by the Act just mentioned, and provided that any lands in the Rainy River District considered suitable for settlement and cultivation may, by Order in Council, be appropriated as free grants upon the terms specified. Twenty townships have been so appropriated and agents appointed for the sale and location of Crown lands at the following places :—Rainy River, Fort Francis and Rat Portage. (See p. 41). Rat Portage is situated on the line of the Canadian Pacific Railway, distant from Toronto 1,154 miles. From this town, intending settlers on the Rainy River free grants make their way to Fort Francis or other points by steamer on the Lake-of-the-Woods and thence by the Rainy River.

The Rainy River District is the western division of Ontario, bordering on Manitoba, and comprises a large area of the most valuable timber lands in the whole Dominion. The Rainy River itself marks the International boundary line, and its valley, which is the most extensive in the district, is admirably adapted for agriculture, the soil being a rich, alluvial deposit, and considered equal in fertility to the best lands in Manitoba and the North-West. Here are located the townships set apart as free grants, and in addition to a soil that is as rich as the most favoured portions of the western prairies, the settler will have the important advantages of an unlimited supply of wood and water. The river is about eighty miles in length, and the whole of the right, or Canadian bank is covered with a heavy growth of forest trees, shrubs, climbing vines and beautiful flowers. The forests in the district are of immense value, and the lumbering industry which will undoubtedly be prosecuted there on an extensive scale will make farming a profitable undertaking in Rainy River valley. The climate is similar to that of the old settled parts of the Province, and the luxuriance of the vegetation gives evidence of the richness of the soil. All kinds of grain, roots and garden vegetables yield abundant crops, as has been proved by the settlers who have already taken up land in the neighbourhood of Fort Francis, which is situated on the river bank about two miles from Rainy Lake. The name of Alberton has been given to this settlement. It has been organized as a municipality embracing a territory of eighteen miles along the river bank and ten miles back, including the townships of Crozier and Lash.

ALGOMA DISTRICT.

By its intersection with railways and colonization roads the District of Algoma has acquired convenient means of access to outside markets and is now attracting public attention, not only on account of the mining and lumbering operations carried on within its borders, but also because of its millions of acres of valuable lands which offer a most desirable field for the profitable pursuit of stock raising, as well as general farming. It contains several of the free grant townships, many townships not yet open for settlement, besides large tracts of government lands on sale to actual settlers at twenty cents per acre, and a considerable portion of these lands is of excellent quality and well fitted for the purposes mentioned. Among its advantages as a stock raising country are an abundant supply of water—creeks, springs, rivers and lakes being plentifully distributed throughout the entire district ; absence of summer droughts and consequent abundance of green pasture, from the disappearance of the snow in spring till its falling at the beginning of winter ; luxuriant hay and root crops and a fertility of soil which in some localities is not excelled in any other part of the Province. For cattle ranching there are special facilities in the lands stretching along the river banks, while on the high lands and rocky bluffs and ridges, sheep can be pastured without cost through the spring, summer and autumn seasons.

A miller who removed from Eastern Ontario to the Algoma District some years ago, writes :—

"I feel satisfied that Algoma is fully equal to Eastern Ontario for mixed farming. All kinds of grain do well here. Grass can not be beaten, we can raise better grassfed beef in Algoma than can be produced in any part of Ontario (or Canada). As for grain I never milled better wheat than I have done in Algoma. I made quite a number of tests from farmers' grists during the winter, and seldom found a test go below sixty pounds per bushel, and some as high as sixty-five pounds per bushel. For the vicinity of Port Lock, on the North Shore between Bruce Mines and Sault Ste. Marie, spring wheat averages from twenty to twenty-five bushels per acre, fall or winter wheat twenty-five to thirty bushels per acre. Pease are easily grown and are a sure crop. They average about forty bushels per acre. Oats are generally a good crop. All kinds of root crops grow well here. I have known potatoes to yield fifty bushels from one bushel planted."

A farmer residing near Sault Ste. Marie, who came from Norfolk, England, and has spent over twelve years in Algoma, says :—

"A man coming here without any money, if he works hard and has a knowledge of the business, can perhaps get on better in Algoma than in other countries where there is no work or employment in the winter months as there is in Algoma in the woods and mines and on public works ; but the kind of farmers to come here, and the men who would make themselves independently well off in a very short time, are tenant farmers and others with a little means or capital and a good practical knowledge of farming or stock raising, men who understand it as a business and who have a little money to buy good stock and implements and get well started."

OPINIONS OF THE BRITISH FARMER DELEGATES.

That this Province has special attractions for the tenant farmer of the United Kingdom who finds his labours unremunerative and his capital shrinking, has been acknowledged by eminent practical authorities. Professor Sheldon, who from careful observation has a thorough knowledge of the condition of agriculture in Ontario, recognizes this fact, and specially recommends this Province to the British tenant farmer seeking a new field and better returns for his investments. The advanced system of farming for the carrying on of which Ontario, of all the Provinces, offers the most admirable facilities, the geographical position of the Province, the material and social surroundings, all conspire to make the change from the old to the new world one in which the advantages altogether outweigh the inconveniences. This conclusion did not fail to impress itself upon the tenant-farmer delegates who, on the invitation of the High Commissioner, visited Canada in 1890, "to report " upon its agricultural resources and the advantages the country offers " for the settlement of farmers and farm labourers and the other classes " for which there is a demand." The reports of these gentlemen have been printed and widely circulated, and all of them who have expressed an opinion discriminating between the Provinces have recognized that for certain classes of intending emigrants Ontario offers the most favourable and promising field. A few extracts from these reports are here appended :—

Mr. Wm. Edwards, of Ruthin, Wales, says :—

" The Province of Ontario, which is the oldest in the Dominion except Quebec and Nova Scotia, has much the same appearance as the British Isles, but lacks the trim aspect of our quickthorn fences. . . . . . . Many of our most scientific and practical farmers would do well here, and could buy the best farms, with excellent homesteads in thorough repair, for £9 to £15 per acre, or less by paying cash. Money is scarce, and the interest would be high. If a mortgage were required, the rate is from 5½ to 7 per cent., according to the amount and time for which it is required. At first the charge appears high, but when we come to consider that £100 in the hands of a practical man in Canada will go further than £300 in Great Britain, it will be seen that the small capitalist has a much better chance of getting on, and only pays interest equal to 3 per cent. here."

Mr. George Hutchinson, of Brougham Castle, Penrith, says :—

" It appears to me that the English farmer, in taking up land in the older provinces, will find life more like that he has been accustomed to, and will be able to bring the soil into a better state of cultivation in many cases in which it has been much neglected. On the other hand, no one could be better adapted than the native Canadian to open up a new country."

Mr. William Scotson, of Ross Lane, Mossley Hill, Liverpool, after expressing his thanks to the Ontario Minister of Agriculture for courtesies received, says :—

" I think, further, that I am justified in saying that Ontario has sown the seeds of most of the farming now practised in the Dominion west of Ontario, and that she may still be called the premier province for stock and mixed agriculture."

Mr. John T. Wood, of The Court, Halewood, near Liverpool, has the following :—

" There has been for some years a great movement of the younger farmers and farmers' sons from Ontario to Manitoba and the North-West, resulting in a considerable depreciation in the value of farming-land in this o'der province. I have no doubt they will do better in their new homes from a monetary point of view, as they are usually intelligent, shrewd, hard-working men, who make good settlers, and who start out with the intention to succeed. It is very easy, however, to conceive that there are very many Englishmen, who can no longer be described as young men, who have enjoyed considerable comforts at home, contemplating emigration, who should weigh well the advantages Ontario offers in its climate, in the present reasonable terms on which good lands can be acquired, and in the similarity of farming operations generally, with those they have been accustomed to at home. I look upon the present prices of land in this province as tempting ; and I shall be much surprised, indeed, if there is not an appreciation in the value of most of the best farms, which now range from £25 or £30 per statute acre for good lands, well situated, and possessing a desirable and comfortable house and fair buildings, down to £2 per acre for those having few improvements, and only a portion of the area of which has been brought under cultivation."

Col. Francis Fane, of Fulbeck Hall, Grantham, says that it must remain with the emigrant himself where to settle, but were he to give advice, it would be on the following lines : –

" 1. A man with a certain amount of capital could buy a nice farm, with good house and cleared land, at about $30 (£6) an acre, in the Eastern Townships, and many parts of Quebec and Ontario. By doing so, he would avoid the hardships of Manitoba and the North-West ; he would be in the midst of comparative comfort and society, and within easy reach of markets, schools, etc."

Mr. Robert Pitt, of Crickett Court, Ilminster, says :—

" If that part of Canada called the North-West is, so to speak, a good ' settling ground ' for farm or other labourers or for those with little ready money to start with, the older, more thickly populated, and more socially advanced parts in Ontario and the Maritime Provinces are just the places for young, well-educated farmers possessed of some means. Do not, though, let anyone make a grievous mistake by buying a farm for seven or eight hundred pounds as soon as he arrives because it appears cheap ; he will never regret a year's work on someone else's farm, and then, when he is comfortably settled on a well-chosen and much-thought-over place of his own, he will look back on that year of work, with good wages, with pride for the rest of his life, and may be able at middle age to hand on the farm with complacency to a son.

" For those dairymen, or dairy-farmers, as the term applies in different parts of Britain, there appears to be abundant opportunity in Canada. Hard-working people such as these, placed near a good dairy factory in a favourable part of the country, should attain a competence in a few years."

Mr. Henry Simmons, of Bearwood Farm, Workingham, gives some excellent advice to certain classes of intending emigrants, and adds :—

" Another plan, and to many emigrants with capital at command I would very strongly recommend it, would be to go into the Province of Ontario, which embrace an area of 182,000 square miles—much of it very productive land—and seek out one of the many desirable farms constantly to be bought at from £10 to £20 an acre, with good houses, buildings, and fences, and land all under cultivation, and where every comfort of life can be obtained and enjoyed just as easily and more economically than in England."

Mr. George Brown, of Watten Mains, Caithness, thus sets forth the special advantages offered by Ontario to the old country tenant farmer :—

" There can be no doubt, Southern and Western Ontario offer great inducements for old country farmers with some means to settle there instead of moving further west. By so doing they obviate the necessity of " roughing it," and settle down in the midst of a community far advanced in the comforts and luxuries of life. Life is too short for a man of middle age to go into the bush and chop his way to a farm of a couple of hundred acres—all the more when he can buy an improved farm at a reasonable figure ; this can be readily done just now, as many of the pioneers whose families are now grown up are inclined to move west for the sake of the boys."

SETTLER'S EQUIPMENT.

In order to make a successful commencement upon a free grant the settler should have from £60 to £100 ($300 to $500) to buy provisions, building material, stock, implements, etc. But immigrants on their arrival in the country are advised to go out first for a year or more as agricultural labourers. The experience thus acquired will far more than compensate for the time lost. The residents are always willing to help new comers. A house, such as is required by the Act, can be erected by contract for from £8 to £10 ($40 to $50) ; but with the assistance that would certainly be received from neighbours it might be erected for less. The best season of the year to go on to a free grant in the Rainy River valley is April or May, and in the other free grant districts, September or early in the fall after harvest work in the old settlements is over. This will give time to put up a house and get comfortably settled before the winter sets in, and during the winter the work of chopping and clearing can go on. A crop can be got in during the following spring. The operation of putting in the first crop is a very simple one. Ploughing is at once impracticable and unnecessary. The land is light and rich. All it needs is a little scratching on the surface with a drag or harrow to cover the seed.

FARM LABOURERS AND DOMESTIC SERVANTS.

The attractions of Ontario are but faintly represented to the British agricultural labourer by the increased rate of wages his services will command. It is not so much because the wages are better, as because the road to independence is much shorter and far more easy to travel, that he is invited to consider the advantages to be gained by emigrating to this Province. Here after some years of work in the service of others, he can have saved enough to enable him to commence on his own account, a prospect which is placed entirely beyond his reach by the existing conditions at home, and which to one who desires to be his own master should be a sufficient inducement to make him cross the Atlantic.

From the beginning of April till the end of October farm labourers, especially single men, are in constant requisition, the demand during the season of 1892 having been very much in excess of the supply. A single man who can plough well, milk and take care of stock, will readily obtain employment at from $150 to $180 per annum with board. The average rate of wages throughout the Province in 1890 was $157 with, and $253 without board for the year. For youths and young men without experience, the yearly rate ranges from $75 to $120 with board. Employment on the farm in the winter months is rather scarce, but competent men arriving in the spring are eagerly sought for at rates varying from $15 to $20 per month till the first of November ; and youths during the same period command from $8 to $15, in each case with board.

Farm labourers with families can find ready employment if they are experienced and have the means of providing a little furniture and provisions. If there are young women in the family, able and willing to take places as servants, so much the better.

The demand for female domestic servants is constant everywhere throughout the Province at all seasons of the year. The rate of wages for experienced servants ranges from $6 to $12 per month with board. Good general servants can readily find employment at from $7 to $10 per month on their arrival. Young women, however, who are not able or willing to work will not succeed in the Province.

Full information regarding all matters connected with immigration, will be furnished on application, personally or by letter, to

DAVID SPENCE,
Secretary, Immigration Department.
Old Parliament Buildings, Front Street West,
TORONTO, ONT.

Or to

PETER BYRN ,
Nottingham Buildings, 19 Brunswick St.,
LIVERPOOL, ENGLAND.

---

www.ingramcontent.com/pod-product-compliance
Lightning Source LLC
Chambersburg PA
CBHW021554270326
41931CB00009B/1208